Killer Disasters

TORNADOES

Doreen Gonzales

PowerKiDS press
New York

Published in 2013 by The Rosen Publishing Group, Inc.
29 East 21st Street, New York, NY 10010

First Edition

Editor: Amelie von Zumbusch
Book Design: Greg Tucker

Photo Credits: Cover Willoughby Owen/Flickr/Getty Images; p. 4 Todd Shoemake/Shutterstock.com; p. 5 Terry Underwood Evans/Shutterstock.com; pp. 6–7, 15 Melanie Metz/Shutterstock.com; p. 8 Mike Theiss/National Geographic/Getty Images; pp. 9 (left), 19 Jim Reed/Photo Researchers/Getty Images; p. 9 (right) DarkOne/Shutterstock.com; pp. 10, 11 Dustie/Shutterstock.com; p. 13 © Associated Press; pp. 12–13 Melissa Brandes/Shutterstock.com; p. 14 Greg Latza/AFP/Getty Images; p. 16 Deshakalyan Chowdhury/AFP/Getty Images; p. 17 Gavin Averill/Getty Images; p. 18 Tom Pennington/Getty Images; pp. 20–21 Photo Researchers/Getty Images; p. 22 © iStockphoto.com/Steve Shepard.

Library of Congress Cataloging-in-Publication Data

Gonzales, Doreen.
Tornadoes / by Doreen Gonzales. – 1st ed.
p. cm. – (Killer disasters)
Includes index.
ISBN 978-1-4488-7439-2 (library binding) – ISBN 978-1-4488-7512-2 (pbk.) –
ISBN 978-1-4488-7586-3 (6-pack)
1. Tornadoes–Juvenile literature. I. Title.
QC955.2.G66 2013
363.34'923–dc23

2011049715

Manufactured in the United States of America

CPSIA Compliance Information: Batch #B3S12PK: For Further Information contact Rosen Publishing, New York, New York at 1-800-237-9932

CONTENTS

TWISTING AND TURNING

Gray clouds roll across the sky. Suddenly one dips low, spinning and narrowing into a tube. It waves back and forth and reaches toward the ground. The tube moves forward, whirling, swirling, and kicking up dust. This is a tornado! A tornado is a spinning column of air that touches the ground.

This tornado formed on the border between Oklahoma and Colorado. The storm that made the tornado also dropped lumps of ice, called hail.

On April 27, 2011, a big tornado destroyed this gas station in Tuscaloosa, Alabama.

Most tornadoes are small and weak. Some, though, can be 1 mile (2 km) wide and spin at speeds of more than 300 miles per hour (483 km/h). Tornadoes can pull trees right out of the ground and pick up entire buildings. Tornadoes can even kill people.

THE RIGHT STUFF

Most big tornadoes form in thunderstorms. These may form when there is a layer of warm air near the ground and a layer of cool air above that. The warm air rises and cools into water droplets, making a cloud. Then more warm air moves in. That air rises, too. Winds form when it hits the cold air.

Sometimes these winds blow at different speeds and in different directions. The right mix of winds can make the air start spinning in a **horizontal**, or side-to-side, tube. At times, the tube turns **vertical**, or going up and down. If the vertically spinning tube touches the ground, it is a tornado.

This is the kind of thunderstorm that can cause tornadoes.

ROPES, WEDGES, AND WATERSPOUTS

There are several kinds of tornadoes. Long, narrow tornadoes are sometimes called rope tornadoes. **Wedge tornadoes** are wide and cone shaped. Huge thunderstorms called **supercells** create the strongest tornadoes on Earth. These are sometimes known as supercell tornadoes.

Wedge tornadoes look wider than they are tall.

Left: Landspouts, such as this one, are small tornadoes that form without big thunderclouds nearby. They are also called dust-tube tornadoes. *Right*: In the United States, waterspouts are most common in the summer.

A **multivortex tornado** has two or more tornadoes spinning around one center. The winds of the smaller tornadoes can be stronger than those of the larger cloud. Because of this, multivortex tornadoes sometimes destroy one building while leaving the building next to it standing.

Waterspouts are tornadoes that form over warm water. Some are strong enough to turn over boats. Waterspouts sometimes move onto land and become tornadoes.

PATH OF RUIN

In May 2011, one of the deadliest tornadoes in US history tore through Joplin, Missouri. This multivortex tornado formed in Kansas. It then moved east, gaining strength as it moved. By the time it entered Joplin, its winds were blowing at 200 miles per hour (322 km/h).

The Joplin tornado caused a lot of damage. It formed at 5:34 p.m. and lasted until 6:12 p.m.

The 2011 tornado destroyed much of Joplin, including its high school, seen here.

The tornado roared through the city, crushing cars and tossing buses. It knocked over trees and blew buildings apart. It took under an hour for the tornado to pass through Joplin. It destroyed nearly everything in a 6-mile- (10 km) long path.

Disaster in Joplin!

Date:	May 22, 2011
EF scale rating:	EF-5
Maximum path width:	1 mile (2 km)
Path length:	22 miles (35 km)

Lightning flashing inside the Joplin tornado

Homes destroyed:	**6,954**
Cost of property damage:	**More than $2 billion**
Injuries:	**More than 1,000**
Deaths:	**162**

TORNADO ALLEY

The United States has about 1,000 tornadoes each year. This is more than any other country. Most US tornadoes occur in an area called Tornado Alley.

Tornado Alley stretches across the Great Plains from Minnesota to Texas. The land there is very flat. Cold air from Canada can flow across it quite easily. At the same time, warm, moist air from the Gulf of Mexico can easily move north.

These people lived through a tornado that hit Spencer, South Dakota, in 1998. Sadly, the tornado killed six people. Spencer is in Tornado Alley.

This tornado formed near Stuart, Nebraska. Nearly all of Nebraska is in Tornado Alley.

When the cold air meets the warm air, large thunderstorms often form. Many times, these storms produce tornadoes. Tornadoes are most common in Tornado Alley in the late spring.

OUTSIDE THE ALLEY

Tornadoes form in places outside Tornado Alley, too. For example, the southeastern United States has many tornadoes each year. Tornadoes also strike in other countries. For example, Australia has many tornadoes.

This woman's home in northeastern India was destroyed in a tornado. The village she lives in is in the part of India that is near Bangladesh.

A tornado destroyed these buildings in Atlanta, Georgia. The parts of the southeastern United States that are often hit by tornadoes are known as Dixie Alley.

Some of the strongest tornadoes outside the United States occur in south central Bangladesh. This is a place where cold air comes across flat land to meet warm, moist air from the Bay of Bengal. Tornadoes are a special danger to the people who live in this area. Many of their homes are made of mud and straw. Each year, the tornadoes that strike this area cause many deaths.

How Strong Is It?

Scientists **estimate** the strength of a tornado by figuring out its wind speed. They do this by seeing how much damage it has caused. They then rate the tornado on the Enhanced Fujita scale.

In 2011, an EF-4 tornado destroyed this woman's home and business in Tuscaloosa, Alabama.

The Enhanced Fujita Scale

EF Number	3-Second Gust Speed
0	65–85 mph (105–137 km/h)
1	86–110 mph (138–177 km/h)
2	111–135 mph (179–217 km/h)
3	136–165 mph (219–266 km/h)
4	166–200 mph (267–322 km/h)
5	Over 200 mph (Over 322 km/h)

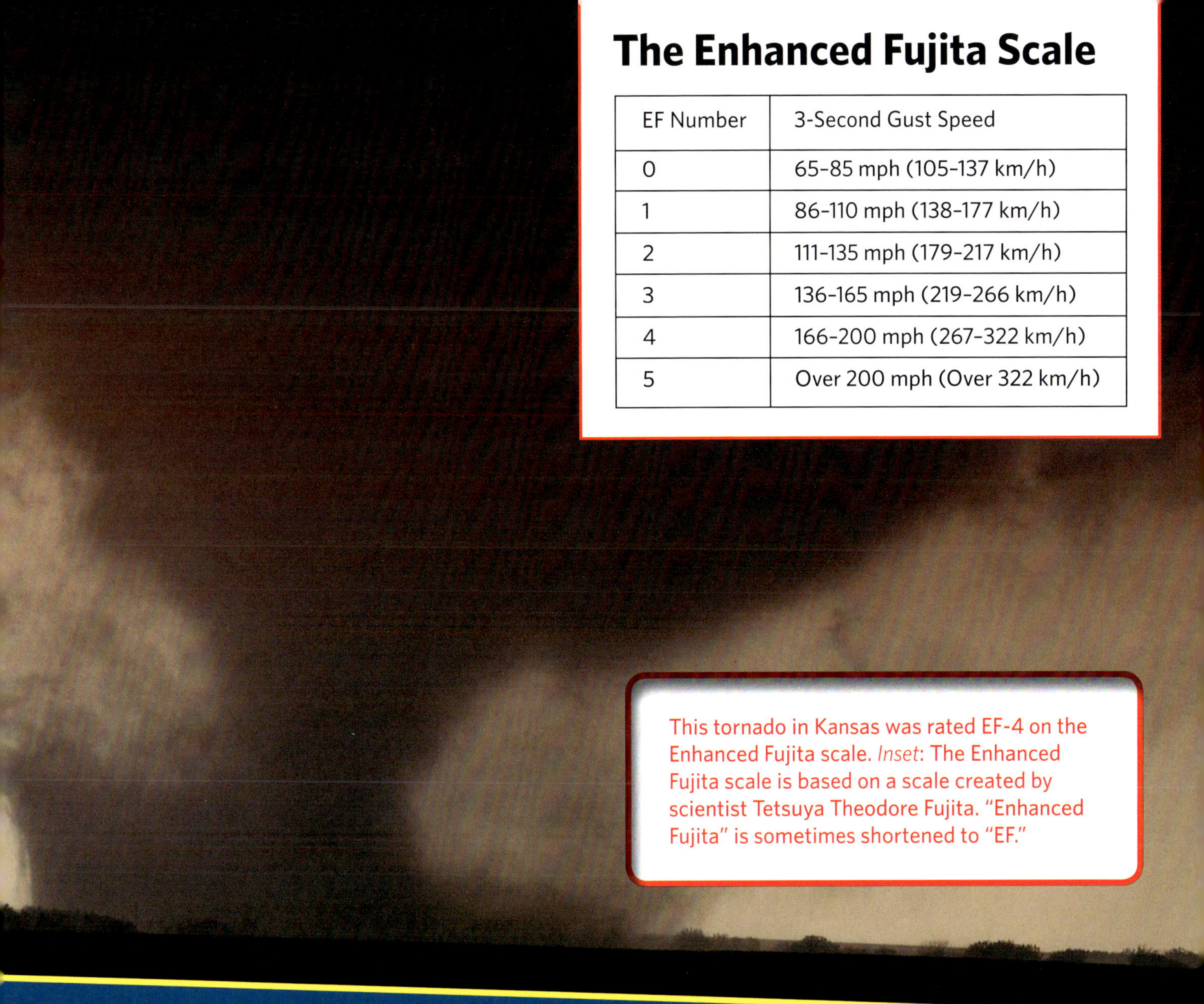

This tornado in Kansas was rated EF-4 on the Enhanced Fujita scale. *Inset*: The Enhanced Fujita scale is based on a scale created by scientist Tetsuya Theodore Fujita. "Enhanced Fujita" is sometimes shortened to "EF."

An EF-0 tornado is the weakest kind of tornado. It can break tree branches and damage signs. It has winds from 65 to 85 miles per hour (105–137 km/h). An EF-3 tornado can rip roofs off of houses.

The strongest tornadoes are rated EF-5. An EF-5 tornado can tear sturdy houses from the ground and toss cars around. Its winds blow at more than 200 miles per hour (322 km/h).

Storm Chasing

Scientists want to become better at **predicting** tornadoes. They study them using a tool called **Doppler radar**. It measures spinning winds. Sometimes scientists make tornadoes in special rooms, or **chambers**, to see how they behave.

People called storm chasers drive to thunderstorms in case a tornado forms. They want to be as close as possible to measure its **temperatures** and winds. Some people fly airplanes into storms to gather information.

Scientists use all of this information to build **computer models** of storms that make tornadoes. Then, when a new storm forms, the models can tell them if it might make a tornado.

Storm chasers get to see tornadoes up close. However, chasing tornadoes can be unsafe. It is not something kids should do.

Be Smart and Stay Safe

Scientists at the National Weather Service watch for tornadoes. When they think one might form, they send warnings to news stations.

If a tornado is predicted near you, move to a basement. If you have no basement, go to a bathroom or closet in the middle of the house. Stay away from windows. If you are outside, get in a car. If you know what to do when a tornado appears, you can keep yourself safe!

Some places have shelters where people can hide during a tornado. Shelters tend to be underground.

GLOSSARY

CHAMBERS (CHAYM-burz) Rooms.

COMPUTER MODELS (kum-PYOO-ter MAH-dulz) Computer programs that show what might happen in real life.

DOPPLER RADAR (DAH-plur RAY-dar) A tool that uses sound waves to track storms.

ESTIMATE (ES-teh-mayt) To make a guess based on knowledge or facts.

HORIZONTAL (hor-ih-ZON-til) Going from side to side.

MULTIVORTEX TORNADO (mul-tee-VOR-teks tor-NAY-doh) Two or more tornadoes spinning around one center.

PREDICTING (prih-DIK-ting) Making a guess based on facts or knowledge.

SUPERCELLS (SOO-per-selz) The largest, strongest thunderstorms.

TEMPERATURES (TEM-pur-cherz) How hot or cold things are.

VERTICAL (VER-tih-kul) In an up-and-down direction.

WATERSPOUTS (WAH-ter-spowts) Tornadoes that happen over lakes or oceans.

WEDGE TORNADOES (WEJ tawr-NAY-dohz) Tornadoes that look as wide as they are tall.

INDEX

WEBSITES

Due to the changing nature of Internet links, PowerKids Press has developed an online list of websites related to the subject of this book. This site is updated regularly. Please use this link to access the list: www.powerkidslinks.com/kd/torn/